Domes

A Frank O'Hara Award Book

Domes

John Koethe

Published for
The Frank O'Hara Foundation
at Columbia University Press
New York and London 1973

Some of these poems have appeared in the following magazines: *Adventures in Poetry:* "Some"; *The Falcon:* "Song"; *Fire Exit:* "The Hand in the Breast Pocket"; *49 South:* "Belgium," "Punchinellos and Dancing Dogs"; *The Harvard Advocate:* "Sodden"; *Juillard:* "Seascape with Clouds and Birds"; *Mulberry:* "Tourmaline"; *Panache:* "Natural Knowledge"; *Paris Review:* "A Sunday Drive," "Copley Square"; *Poetry:* "Domes," "Mission Bay," "Personal Life," "Process," "Satie's Suits," "Summer," "Tiny Figures in Snow"; *Quarterly Review of Literature:* "Below the Coast," "Bird," "Level," "Maps," "Men and Wives," "Power and Persuasion." Also, in *Blue Vents* (Audit/Poetry, 1969); and in the anthologies *Another World* (Bobbs-Merrill, 1971) and *Ten American Poets* (Carcanet, 1973).

Some of the lines in the poem "Men and Wives" are taken from Ivy Compton-Burnett's novel of the same title.

Library of Congress Cataloging in Publication Data

Koethe, John, 1945–
 Domes.

 Poems.
  1. Frank O'Hara Foundation. II. Title.
PS3561.035D6 811'.5'4 73-4289
ISBN 0-231-03743-0
ISBN 0-231-03744-9 (pbk)

For Susan

THE 1972 FRANK O'HARA AWARD FOR POETRY

The annual Frank O'Hara Award for Poetry, named for the American poet who was killed in 1966, was established by the Frank O'Hara Foundation to encourage the writing of experimental poetry and to aid in its publication. The award is meant to carry on in some measure Frank O'Hara's interest in helping new poets in their work. Eligible for it are poets who have not had a book of poetry published or accepted for publication by a commercial or university press. Further information about the award is available from the Frank O'Hara Foundation, 145 West 45th Street, New York, New York 10036. Columbia University Press, for the Foundation, published in 1968, *Spring in This World of Poor Mutts*, by Joseph Ceravolo; in 1969, *Highway to the Sky*, by Michael Brownstein; in 1970, *North*, by Tony Towle; and in 1971, *Motor Disturbance*, by Kenward Elmslie.

The winner of the 1972 Frank O'Hara Award for Poetry is John Koethe, who was born in San Diego, California, in 1945. He graduated from Princeton and has recently completed his work for a doctorate in philosophy at Harvard. Mr. Koethe's poems have appeared in a variety of magazines and anthologies, and he has published one book of poetry, *Blue Vents* (Audit/Poetry, 1969). He has also written art criticism for *Art News* and literary criticism for *Poetry* and *Parnassus*. He is married and is teaching at the University of Wisconsin in Milwaukee.

The design for the jacket of the clothbound edition and the cover of the paperbound edition of this book is by Fairfield Porter.

Contents

Domes

Song

I used to like getting up early
(I had to anyway) when the light was still smoky
And before the sun had finished burning the fog away.
The sun rose behind a cool yellow mountain

I could see through my window, and its first rays
Hit a funny looking bump on the wall next to my head.
I would look at it for a little while and then get up.
Meanwhile, something was always doing in the kitchen,

For every day took care of itself:
It was what I got dressed for, and then it moved away
Or else it hung around waiting for someone to turn
Saying "I thought so." But it always ended.

—I know it's hopeless remembering,
The memories only coming to me in my own way, floating
          around like seeds on the wind
Rustling in the leaves of the eucalyptus tree each morning,
The texture of light and shade. They feel the same, don't
          they,

All these memories, and each day seems,
Like one in high school, a distraction from itself
Prefaced only by one of a few dreams, resembling each other
Like parts of the same life, or like the seasons.

1

Come spring you'd see lots of dogs
And summer was the season when you got your hair cut off.
It rained a little more in winter, but mostly,
Like autumn, one season resembled the next

And just sat there, like the mountain with the "S" on it,
Through weather every bit as monotonous as itself.
And so you'd lie in bed, wondering what to wear that day,
Until the light mended and it was time to get ready for
        school.

—Is there anything to glean from these dumb memories?
They let you sleep for a while, like Saturday,
When there was nothing you were supposed to do.
But it doesn't seem enough just to stay there,

Close to the beginning,
Rubbing your eyes in the light, wondering what to wear now,
        what to say:
Like the eternal newcomer with his handkerchief and his
        lunchpail,
Looking around, and then sliding away into the next dream.

2

The House

If the sun were huge, or not round,
Or quick enough to encircle the earth
Like a band, perhaps we could understand
Their horror of light:
The eyeball covered with a spoon;
Thick beams laid over the face.

This is the house of the last boy.
Each moment discloses a room
No memory can invade, a fixed space
Where all dreams are equal. Never ask:

What have you done with the trains?
But: The men who met here before the trains
Began to exist, what have you done with *them?*
Who can see them in the bricks and bilge,
The careful volumes of our hearts?

The mouth torn down
By a blade. The easy meeting
Of friends on a porch.
The clouds move expertly across the sky,
But the kitten sees, or through her eyes we see

The body fail of its own nature, until only
In speech or only in mobs can it move
As it wants to, conscious of being watched
By us, from a room in the country.

Below the Coast

A clumsy hillock
Unmolded like a cake on the meadow
In the Laguna Mountains. Tough yellow-green grass growing
            up to a tree
As thick as a tooth. In winter, on the road from San Diego,
Thousands of cars crawl up to the snow
And their passengers get out to investigate it
And then drive, discoursing, back home. And that's Califor-
            nia,
Solemnly discharging its responsibilities.

Meanwhile we breakfast on pancakes the size of a plate
While the console radio goes on the blink.
Miss L'Espagnole looks out from her frame on the wall,
Completely prepared (though for what it is impossible to
            say).
Her left arm is white and dips into a puddle of fire
Or a pile of cotton on fire. And each thing is severe:
The house hemmed in by pepper trees and Mexico
(This one is white and in Chula Vista), and the paraphernalia
Strewn around home: a few magazines summing up politics,
A matchbox with a lavender automobile on the cover,
And a set of soldiers of several military epochs marching off
            to war on the raffia rug.
Unless you've grown up amidst palm trees (and buildings
            that are either unbuilt, or hospitals)
It's impossible to appreciate a reasonable tree.

I sometimes consider the parrots that live in the zoo
And are sold on the street in Tijuana. Colored like national flags,
Their heads are always cocked to pick up something behind them.

And unless you have lived in a place where the fog
Closes in like a face, it is impossible to be (even temporarily)
relieved
When it lifts to expose the freshly painted trim of the city,
and it seems
Like a fine day for knowledge: sunlight sleeping on top of the
rocks
And lots of white clouds scudding by like clean sheets,
Which, when the air in the bedroom is cold, you pull over
your head
And let the temperature slowly increase while you breathe.
But California has only a coast in common with this.

5

Maps

Maps are a guide to good conduct.
They will not go away from your life,
But in return, they promise you safety
And entertain you with political visions.

As investments in the commonplace
The cowboy and mystic alike both need trains—
Formulaic, impersonal trains,
Warmed by the engineer's tears.

Theirs is a history of polite good sense
Yet it has the perfect confidence of a dream.
Now nothing can alter your body,
But the dream changes when you go away

And information arises to take its place.
Carried from place to arrival,
Operating on a program of intense change,
You seem a part of the lives of those near you

But the horizon is made of expensive steel
That dopes you with a sort of elastic energy
Like a particular spot in the brain.
He is a precision-made man

Whose life is a series of privileged instants,
Examples—like greeting or going away.
But who can remember old entertainment?
The couple locked in a good hotel,

The hotel locked with a profound happiness.
Outside, the forest. These maps
Prevent sadness, but really are nothing but history
Of simple encounter, or dreams and geometrical charms.

They are samples. They move in the light.
The light continues to move in the eye
Of a sleeping man. A tremendous hint
Falls over the station: the man is about to be killed.

At best he will be permitted to live in an old mine.
The girl evaporates in back of a city official
And in the mirror the boy holds up his hands
To cover his face. Anyway, nobody comes.

Where are the acts you tried to conceal
Like a hand you put away somewhere and forgot?
The spirit died when the man went into the cave
But see what these maps have done with your hand.

Process

Like that definite thing
I'd postponed, calling you
The sky's clear streak facing
The porch—how can my emotions be
So thin, and so lately recognized?
You remind me. Chords of you slumber fitfully

Tossing the bottled logic swans and
Imperial necks, vases, counterpoints
The lightning silent but "edgy."
This room must have a past,
I am living in it.
Here the rain though discontinued
Comes out like thunder—that baffles
You, and your innocence that I invent.

Level

Eventually, I'd hoped, I would please you.
I would call you the right names,
Bend with your gestures, remember your actions,
Extracting them gladly, but within real limits.

I see I was wrong. Shall I find you different,
Easy, supple, and without pain?
Or is energy part of the music?
I try. I am trying to ask you.

O the noises that cannot be touched!
The faces have passed me like a brown dream

For how can they change?
Always unbearably tender, and constant,
Like a house that is tender and constant.

You are like other people. There is,
I suppose, no reason to want you
Unless desire itself is a reason, drawing us
Out of our kindness, leaving us terrified

Peace. Beauty, we know,
Is the center of fear, hammering,
Holding in a loose ring your purposeful
Dream—and you see them

Looking painfully into your face, though you know
They will never come back in the same way.

Domes

for John Godfrey

1. Animals

Carved—indicated, actually—from solid
Blocks of wood, the copper-, cream-, and chocolate-colored
Cows we bought in Salzburg form a tiny herd.
    And in Dr. Gachet's etching, six
Or seven universal poses are assumed by cats.

Misery, hypocrisy, greed: a dying
Mouse, a cat, and a flock of puzzled blackbirds wearing
Uniforms and frock coats exhibit these traits.
    Formally outlasting the motive
Of their creation with a poetry at once too vague

And too precise to do anything with but
Worship, they seem to have just blundered into our lives
By accident, completely comprehending
    Everything we find so disturbing
About them; but they never speak. They never even move

From the positions in which Grandville or some
Anonymous movie-poster artist has left them,
A sort of ghostly wolf, a lizard, an ape
    And a huge dog. And their eyes, looking
At nothing, manage to see everything invisible

To ours, even with all the time in the world
To see everything we think we have to see. And tell
Of this in the only way we really can:
    With a remark as mild as the air
In which it is to be left hanging; or a stiff scream,

Folded like a sheet of paper over all
The horrible memories of everything we were
Going to have. That vanished before our eyes
    As we woke up to nothing but these,
Our words, poor animals whose home is in another world.

2. Summer Home

Tiny outbursts of sunlight play
On the tips of waves that look like tacks
Strewn upon the surface of the bay.
Up the coast the water backs up
Behind a lofty, wooded island. Here,
According to photographs, it is less
Turbulent and blue; but much clearer.
It seems to exercise the sunlight less
Reflecting it, allowing beaten silver sheets
To roam like water across a kitchen floor.
Having begun gradually, the gravel beach
Ends abruptly in the forest on the shore.

Looked at from a distance, the forest seems
Haunted. But safe within its narrow room
Its light is innocent and green, as though
Emerging from another dream of diminution
We found ourselves of normal, human size,
Attempting to touch the leaves above our heads.
Why couldn't we have spent our summers here,
Surrounded and growing up again? Or perhaps
Arrive here late at night by car, much later
In life? If only heaven were not too near
For such sadness. And not within this world
Which heaven has finally made clear.

Green lichen fastened to a blue rock
Like a map of the spot; cobwebs crowded with stars
Of water; battalions of small white flowers.
Such clarity, unrelieved except by our
Delight and daily acquiescence in it,
Presumably the effect of a natural setting
Like this one, with all its expectations of ecstasy
And peace, demands a future of forgetting
Everything that sustains it: the dead leaves
Of winter; the new leaves of spring which summer burns
Into different kinds of happiness; for these,
When autumn drops its tear upon them, turn.

14

3. Domes

"Pleased in proportion to the truth
Depicted by means of familiar images." That
One was dazed; the other I left in a forest
Surrounded by giant, sobering pines.
For I had to abandon those lives.
Their burden of living had become
Mine and it was like dying: alone,
Huddled under the cold blue dome of the stars,
Still fighting what died and so close to myself I could not
    even see.
I kept trying to look at myself. It was like looking into the
    sun and I went blind.

O to break open that inert light
Like a stone and let the vision slowly sink down
Into the texture of things, like a comb flowing through dark,
Heavy hair; and to continue to be affected much later.
I was getting so tired of that excuse: refusing love
Until it might become so closely mated to its birth in
Acts and words of love; until a soft monstrosity of song
Might fuse these moments of affection with a dream of home;
The cold, prolonged proximity of God long after night
Has come and only starlight trickles through the dome;

And yet I only wanted to be happy.
I wanted rest and innocence; a place
Where I could hide each secret fear by blessing it,
By letting it survive inside those faces I could never under-
stand,
Love, or bear to leave. Because I wanted peace, bruised with
prayer
I tried to crawl inside the heavy, slaughtered hands of love
And never move. And then I felt the wound unfold inside me
Like a stab of paradise: explode: and then at last
Exhausted, heal into pain. And that was happiness:
A dream whose ending never ends, a vein

Of blood, a hollow entity
Consumed by consummation, bleeding so.
In the sky our eyes ascend to as they sweep
Upward into emptiness, the angels sing their listless
Lullabies and children wake up glistening with screams
They left asleep; and the dead are dead. The wounded wor-
ship death
And live a little while in love; and then are gone.
Inside the dome the stars assume the outlines of their lives:
Until we know, until we come to recognize as ours,
Those other lives that live within us as our own.

Tourmaline

That building of leaves,
The dusk motes, the intervals
Of alternation and shade
Constituting the soul,
They all seem lifted now.
It is not even very late.
Only hovering over its hopes,
Bouncing its fears on its knee,
The concrete soul seems as in
A world where it is always
Dark or light, or an October day,
Breathless and clear,
Left on the lips like water;
Where what they meant and wanted
Matters. Only somewhere,
Entities, they still do.

Some

Some of them woke up forgetting.
When some of them woke up
We'd already forgotten them for a long time.
We've been reading about each other for a long time.
But I liked it better before,
When there was sun in the sky
And the sky hung upside-down in the water.
Now we all wake up on the same day
And the same light taps the trees:
Everything is closer.
Isn't there anyplace left anymore where we can all be?
"I shall never get this peace, I only know it *exists*."
Still, there ought to be more pleasure in it all—
The light falling over your arms,
The darkness coughing at me.
If I am closed to you now
It is because you are to me—
I hardly speak to you anymore;
You never speak to me
And it hurts to look at you, knowing you think I hate you.
Weren't the days longer once
And the nights almost as long?
There was more to see and do and talk about
And the sun smiled across the sky, broadening each day
Until summer, until the trees talked.
And in winter they were cold and so beautiful.

Now I only look at you and argue.
And yet I like it here—
It barely breathes, but I like this little coastal town with its
        roofs and clouds,
Its ups and downs and corner bakery,
Its tiny sun, so tiny that you can almost hold it in a spoon,
And the light like hair, unbound around the leaves.
This is its song,
Sounding more like it always has than ever,
Even acting the same way:
We do what we're told,
We tell each other about everything we do, until it's hard to
        know who's speaking;
When our fingers touch, they touch the water
And the life flows out through them, into the air.

Domestic Scenes

I want the rain to stop falling down
So I can go out and walk, grandly,
As a white boat floats on a flat lake.

I awaken each day to the same natural laws
That govern the Indian Ocean. Geography:
I try to approach you, and you go to sleep

Or my body deceives me again. Last night
I thought you were here with me.
I gave you to all of my friends

And my friends surrounded me.
Now there is a noise like applause.
The lawnmower cuts down the backyard.

Saints who remember their early temptations
Must re-experience them, and they fall.
The moon reminds them of old pain;

They argue in bedrooms; in palaces, treason . . .
But this sadness is really so accidental.
Someday a breeze will arise to console us

And like a gesture of ease and unaccomplishment
Prosperity will ring from the whole coast.
It will be a coincidence not arranged by chance.

Bird

What bird has read *all* the books?
The crow lives by a passionate insincerity
That means naturalness in an impossible world

And so is a unit by which we can measure ourselves
In the real one. The swallow defines "exact place"
So that we know it exists beyond sight

And the criminal depth of the night sky.
Yet owls never move, flamingoes just
Stand there, victims of the tall trees

And emblems of space or beautiful hair.
Our little canary recalls the first crisis:
Inclined planes, the separate enterprises

Necessary if we are able to exist at all.
The birds cannot reach us.
But we hear the sleeping art of their music

And it hints at all the evaporated experience
We need for our simplest move, our first
Aspiration, "flight." Hummingbirds are just space.

Belgium

Do I want to listen to myself
Or Belgium?

"At first we were miles apart.
Later we drew closer to each other—
Each as the other could bear."
That is how it was in Belgium.

Now as for myself—
You would have to remain with me,
Living in a single place with me
For many years.

So we lived for a long time in Belgium.

"You're surprised when I don't
But you hardly even notice when I do."

Inching off
In a given direction
Many stories under the sky

There is a nominal charge for everything you want to do
In Belgium

Depicted on a postage stamp
These figures vanished into a low sky.

In the Middle

I am miserable shelling peas without you.
But you are magnificent and sunburned.
    "What a beautiful sunburned creature she is"—

The quarreling white cheeses.
    In Wichita Falls, Texas
    I am completely spent, but keep adding
and adding these figures.

What possessed me to sit by the Thames and sleep?

The possession of your eight dancing cylinders.

Salute. You always arrive at those times.

I started a painting but everything
turned into thick "white" paint—
    like the rapids of the supple Colorado.

But these are actually brown, more like mud
or the butter we bought in Topeka.
    I still carry the scars of that luminous summer drizzle
    falling as we emerged with the peaches and figs.
    We were glistening afterwards, but I seldom see you

anymore. We are so simple together and slip
so easily apart. We'd better burn down the villa.

Bring on the savage fruits:
    melons, cherries, knotted raisins,
    oranges, and plump blue grapes.
We taste each other as the vistas of Wednesday converge

on the city like chariots or doves.
    Those were tight times. Loosen me,
    no one has cheated us, our property goes
    for a penny and fullness comes to the suave river.

I was fantastic in Montana—thank you
    for the disorder you have ignited here.
I love the way you move alone out of this place.

24

Natural Knowledge

It ought to be true, not just
A "style of argument," whose details
Can be filled in later, when there is time to relax.
—Which doesn't mean it ought to be completely obvious.
There should be room to look around in,

Something you knew
Before knowing whether you wanted it or not.
—True, the sedentary soul,
Sitting on the porch like an insect
In the shade of some lawn furniture, gets bigger and blanker
Avoiding its favorite phrase.
But wouldn't the pleasure shift its gaze?

Exterior

Like illustrated old autumn,
His information was already common knowledge,
For the prayer that had made him return to the farms
Had just become used, and being everywhere

Simultaneous, indifferent. But whether this lesson
Merely circulated as a legend in life or not
Was immaterial, for that it should go around praised
And unheeded could only mean it was true.

He is a planet and lives in that fashion.
Like a holiday, always waiting to be withheld,
The rural districts old or new were unaffected
As ever, standing silently aside until called on

To settle the body down on a spot previously
Quiet and unpainted, to be changed into barnyards
Of fact. The rebuke seems indifferent;
The applause the closest thing to a sigh.

For exaggerating even the tiniest threat, he joins
Intimately the satisfied landscape and therefore
Corrupts it . . . he was afraid of so much:
The factory, the whip and the siren,

"The light dove cleaving the air in invisible flight,"
And completely aware of the humor that landed him here
He championed its cause without meaning; like an unsatisfied
        girl
He interpreted gestures as warnings: he could imagine

The sun only as its imagined descent on a county
Of genuine voices and circus cathedrals; or else
Like his calm genuflection that signals the giant's
Steel in the face of a smile, the saddest things in the world.

Sodden

If you thwack him on the head with a spoon
It'll put him out cold.
He won't wake up
Until you arrive at work.

He is starting to stir in your purse.

Now have you ever seen water fall,
Unshaped by container, through about thirty feet
Of air? Just like a jellyfish

Thwack. The sonic boom of thunder
And thick rain starts to come down like a fur
Of water, primarily on the leaves
Of the backyard, jungle-kit trees.

Mary Astor's Journal

The infamous "Blue Diary" of the thirties
At long last purified by fire. Only
In New York could the body be free enough
To completely turn over its passion to words
Too stupid to ever conceal.

"His first initial is 'G'—
"And I fell for him like a ton of bricks."

Arriving by plane in L.A.
She found him but recently dressed,
Arms bare in the rain. "Gosh, it's so
Perfectly hard!" she breathed on her ticket.
And then: "What woman was happier, ever?"

In 1935 Arletta Duncan, the Harvest Queen of Belle Plaine,
Iowa, decided to bow out. She collected all the memorabilia
of her Hollywood career and made a great bonfire in a vacant lot in San Pedro. Then she mounted the gigantic, lethal
letter "H" that was part of a development sign spelling out
HOLLYWOODLAND, and nude, facing the city which had refused
her a crown, flung herself into the air. Her leap landed her
square in a clump of prickly-pear cactus, where she was later
discovered, "a broken body hiding a broken heart"—her tale
typical of many others.

O desert night!
The magician leaves, cruel fire descends.
His final weapon in the showdown:
"I need you," through tears,
Dumbly connecting the words through smoke
Until finally the pleasure is ours.

White Night

I was reading the readings
Dial set at "Coma"

And night looked through the window at
The folded cat

"And now it is all going to be better"

Which soon found us in the garage
Where just as day fell fur flew

Mission Bay

The man-made bay, its fat weeds
Hidden by brack water, which daily
Floats the picnic-papers out to sea;
Divided in two by a thin spit of sand
Drying its back in the sun.
Then the ocean recovers, and the bay
Becomes one flat pond concealing lives
That are just not interested in mine.
In the eyeless eyes of the fish
People from Arizona drive up in white cars,
Suspended like things in a test tube among
The blunt orange buildings lining the shore
Of this bay where I learned how to speak, to
And of myself, by merely repeating the words
With no more distance than the earth can bear.

A Short Account

At least a hundred different magazines
Are visible, but they are written in a Slavic language!
A needle-slim steeple and a red turret
Are visible as well, and some students too,
Shaking with cold on the steps (or steppes).
This is how it all might look to a bird
Suspended, if thought were flight, in flight.

But right now I'd prefer an absence of distance
For a while, to afford my heart a chance to grow
Fonder of all the things it beholds. Like the name
Of a friend, something you don't "remember,"
The soft structure of a cloud, blue-gray
And slowly traversing the width of the sky,
The truth of all that isn't concealed, though it remains
        unheard
—As winter trees, their branches tousled like hair,
Seem to shimmer behind a warm veil of air.

33

Personal Life

If I wake up tired and red or
Symbolic, or if, fevered, my lips
Want to be kissed until they crack, it's just me
Biting the flames to be free, but personal and
Cautious as an eyelid on which the wind dies.

It's fine to create a ruckus indoors
But it's better to go outdoors first
And soak up some weather first-hand
Instead of stirring up a hurricane
Merely to sit in its peaceful eye.

                                      Am I misled
Like the swallow, exploring but coming home empty
Or happy, encumbered with coupons? Heart,
You are too scientific to be accurately wild—
And where is that mild expansive feeling
Lapping over the puddle of my will?

No, I must become diligent like a spouse,
Or I'll be organized like the tree that sits
And sits through the stormy narrative pouring
From the winter blue lips of the city. And I know
What it means to be described: hidden behind glass
Or out under the freckled sky begging for work to
Release me, it is a liberty which breaks, nervous
And selfish as evening, around my knees.

Summer

It's a sooty disgrace—
Four city days of snow and now physics
Turning the page from white into black.
Sears' parking lot is finally open again
To cars from which people emerge only to falter
Headlong into ice and grime.

But can you imagine Boston blown open
Like a delicious orange promise, all wet
And deserving the pressure of our feet,
The hard details of love in the city
Amidst want and taxis, so bravely specific.

    I was going to say it's "enchanting"
    But I'm not sure now . . .
                this sleep—
                is it one of those "facts"
                of literature pulling us away from
                each other in the February dark?

It's so hard to remember the green,
The blue and ordinary persuasions of summer—
Nights that never seem to begin and then continue
Forever, the leaves dried out by the warm wind,
All the empirical information of a June day.
Even then, when the cold eases itself out of life

To fly in a few words into space, I guess some
People continue to dwell in their unremitting holes,
Blind to the reassurance of your face. But there
I find an understanding of love and drudgery
And coffee at seven o'clock in the morning, before
The day wraps us up in its pristine cares that bounce off
Into the cold winter air while under our skins
The small pleasures beat in our blood.

Freedom Trail

The bus, shaped like a package,
Stops in front of Dunkin' Donuts
Long enough for the driver to eat one
Of their damp, underfed donuts and then takes off
Half-empty. Life is acute as a shopping center balloon
Over here, but the tracks the bus crosses take sides
And demand social comment, which the public service
Posters in the bus can't provide:
"Freedom is the price of liberty,"
"Enough is enough," and so on.

At least there's some life in the streets—
Three deckers so close you can feel the rent
Inside of the bus, all gray (ugh!) or green (ugh!),
Covered with tar shingles covered with chips of what
Looks like a sort of colored Kitty Litter,
Evidence of countless cats behind doors.
Silver rain comes down in gray around here, puddles
And soaks the wax out of milk cartons trucks have smashed
Flat. Strange neighborhoods are famous for phone poles,
A sign that we've all somehow "kept in touch" with each other,
So that there can be more wires than sky.

I've got to come here and look for an apartment
As soon as spring starts living up to its reputation.
But now the bus rolls up at the Legal Sea Food Company,
As though emerging from a thicket into a picnic area,
And I get off, glad to have come this way today.

Copley Square

Up-and-down shafts of light brick
Lift occupants up into prisms or roofs
Of green copper, and then embark on the sky.
12:44 by the Suffolk Franklin Savings Bank's
Clock, 93° outside, inside a cool bed of dimes.
A jet overhead that gets picked up by a pigeon
Gliding by lower down, some more modern banks
And a bank of lanterns set like a row of spears.
A Try Rooti Root Beer truck almost collides
With a spiffy yellow Checker Cab, and flags
Flop in front of the Sheraton Plaza Hotel.
Plenty of seersucker walks by below, or sits
On a deep-heated long granite bench,
Listening to the library,
Half-eating a half-eaten peach,
And bakes in the breeze.

A Sunday Drive

Two gallons of apple cider.
A jar of pungent, pasty Yankee mustard.
"Two dollars please." Boys on bikes
Are scattered around the entrance to the store.

Cold leaf smoke floats over
A toadstool-proportioned water tank
Perched slightly off to the left of Route 2.

"Are these houses mostly old or new?
I usually can't tell the difference myself."

So we were continuing down this road
Which was like a hallway whose walls were trees
And whose ceiling was open to the sky.

Large birds were browsing in the sky.

"Her character is slightly slummy
But it conceals a kindness of such concentration
Nothing shivers—not even a single leaf—
When she casts her lot where she may."

Hardly any leaves are left on the trees.
The pines, with their eternal, sickly green,
Are stuck like bottle brushes in the rack
Of the other, occasional bloomers.

"Saws Sharpened."
"The First Lutheran Church Welcomes You."

We can't find the way back, but we do.

Satie's Suits

Orange is the hue of modernity.
Greater than gold, shaky and poetic,
Our century's art has been a gentle surrender
To this color's nonchalant "stance"

Towards hunger and the unknown, and its boldness:
For it has replaced us as the subject of the unknown.
We still like the same things, but today we handle them
    differently.
Among the signs of occupation in this contemporary war

The twelve identical corduroy suits of Erik Satie
Locate importance in repetition, where it really belongs,
There in the dark, among the lessons that sleep excludes.
I want to emphasize the contribution of each one of us

To a society which has held us back but which has
Allowed love to flourish in this age like a song.
Unable to understand very much,
But prepared to isolate things in a personal way,

The acres of orange paint are a sign
Of the machine that powers our amateur hearts.
The technical has been driven back
By river stages, exposing a vacant lot

Strewn with these tools, food and clothing
Awaiting the invention of limited strength.
We could begin selling ourselves, but the overture
Brings no response and the connection remains unsketched.

I can see there has been no change.
The body's a form of remote control
And its success is too exact to assist us.
Responding to the ulterior commandment

So much has failed in the abstract.
The phallus hid in the school bell
While the difficult fluid rose in the night.
In the apartment wild horses took you away.

42

Power and Persuasion

June, its weejuns shoot below the trees.
I was scraping this paste out of my pajamas
Ready for graduation and the big green clot
Of June to come and get in touch with me.
A group of students disappeared in foliage at my feet.

O for a room furnished with a radio
And a complete set of *National Geographic*, so I could grow
        up again.
As though I'd fallen through a telescope into the room,
I felt oversized, too near the people, and their things sur-
        round me,
Like a child who feels older than he really wants to be.

Men and Wives

It's a funny kind of self-effacement:
To burn as fuel for the flame in which others
Are consummated the moment they are consumed,
Brought to bear on the moment:

"And then grow up and be a bride."

There is hardly any setting at all—only enough to insure that
all this is unfolding "somewhere" in particular: amid rocks
and fragrant heather, some "wild thyme unseen," cows,
carved wooden articles. No one influences, or is influenced
by, it; and it is only alluded to once.

For their world would perfect itself
In talk, and in this we are used.
Each night, the struggle to be imitation:
The young man loitering over his microscope,
The boy's feeble reflection of something.
And giving so little of it back to the world,
They were pills, swept away on the physical stream
She could almost remember, or reach.

I always go over and over the same things
To get its inscrutable comment in the vernacular,
Out where you can use it to effect your designs—
Instead of some urge that cannot be canceled in time
And begins by differing, only to turn out familiar.

But I am easier now that you know it
And I am not living alone.

There is supposed to be a model for all this:
The soul's slow progress into annihilation and life
In a body that is able to love people one at a time.

It is the part of the head to be effaced by the hand
As it pauses only to wipe away the smear of some bug
Smashed in the pages when the book on that topic was closed:

Just the empty assertion of fact
And the tears shed over it like rain
Carried away in a hat from which the head is gone.

For the "common ground" is left out
As the details filter down through the wires.
And the innocence of their position brings sadness
To our lives, culminated while they sleep,
Trying to grasp at what they remember.

Anything less than perfection would break down the brain. It is needless to go further when everything has simply to be done.

"I did think something at the time when I used to think. She has some inner grace. To copy her is hopeless. I am on my knees."

"I confess to a preference for bare walls myself. I sound very ungrateful. I know many people prefer a complicated effect."

"There is no definite reason for anxiety, or for expecting to be free of it."

Blue Vents

Will the dwarf ever be able to control
His monstrous need? For he needs cars
As a means to an end—to move
Automatically, freeing his hands
For the tiniest acts: writing on paper
The word "peace," though this is a useless

Peace, based on the useless
Notion that one can control
Objects by closing one's eyes. On paper
It looked good: the quick, low car,
Quiet as the light that falls on the hands
Of a girl combing her hair as she moves

To approach her lover, the way clouds move
Over the city. Everything useless
Was good. And now, sensitive hands,
Needing no further effort to control
Themselves (that was done by the car),
Desired sensation: for instance, the touch of a paper

Clip, placed on the tongue, or a paper
Piano. (But is it possible to move
Brilliantly into ourselves? Can't cars
Also do this, becoming useless,
Beautiful, as soon as we cease to control them?
Can our hands

Remain empty, satisfied just to be hands
Through the wildest night?) Paper
Replaced passion, impossible to control,
But a neuter principle that moved
No one. "We are useless,"
They said, and smiled. The stone cars

Advanced, miserable to be cars,
And as in a circular dream the hand
Dies when the body it wants becomes useless
While giants look on through a paper
Window, so the new clowns moved
Away from what they had never controlled.

What can control our passionate hands?
You laugh. Nothing moves on the paper
But the useless lights of the old cars.

The Friendly Animals

I see that my "voyage of discovery"
Was only a method of continuous sleep.
I have suddenly noticed the vacant chaos
And the mysterious luck that has let me live
Among friendly animals and the other vermin
Who carried knives, short pieces of rope,
Hideous lampshades, cartons of pots and pans
To show me that whatever enters your life
Independently can be put to use later
When there is space in the cabin.

What did their purpose conceal
If not the simplest units of friendship?
Like a ship returning in a foreign language
They have turned into beasts, conscious only
Of one another, blind to perfection,
Finding peace only in each other's arms.

Seascape with Clouds and Birds

for David and Betsy Schatz

The sky around the sun
Is a dense and almost navy blue.
The sand is as white and dry as a white eggshell
And there is a cool wind
Sloshing the ocean around,
Hovering just a few inches above my skin.
When I turn my head
The sun flashes intolerably
And I have to close my eyes.
I could be anywhere.

Where it ends
With a faint surge
And floats across the beach
And then beyond it, and then over the whole world
Before sliding back helplessly,
Some sandpipers, with big flat keys in their backs,
Harass the edge of the sea.
All the other seabirds just squeak.
A pelican falls out of the sky by mistake.

A white seagull floats by
In between white clouds
Which are so small they look like buttons I could run my
        fingers across.

But the sky is a blue cave.
And when I close my eyes
I can see myself standing,
Standing in the deep bowl whose sides I rolled down;
I can see myself on the sand,
Standing in front of the curved waves,
Growing more mean, more horrible.

I am still here.
It feels colder
And it's getting dark
But I can still hear the water—
It sounds like somebody breathing.
And when my eyes squeeze shut
Everything I look at burns with a dark, fabulous flame
And then burns away.
When the breathing stops I want all of this to burn away,

But it never stops
And in a little while,
When the moon is floating through my hands
And everything real enough to change is changing,
I will still be here—
Like a rock, so dense that even the darkness around it burns,
With its soft, wet rock-face open to the air,
And the water, as thick as dreams
And as thin as tears,
Splashing against it.
I am still here.

Tiny Figures in Snow

Cut out of board
And pinned against the sky like stars;
Or pasted on a sheet of cardboard
Like the small gold stars you used to get for being good:
Look at the steeple—
All lit up inside the snow
And yet without a single speck of snow on it.
The more I looked at it, the harder it became to see,
As though I tried to look at something cold
Through something even colder, and could not quite see.
And like the woman in the nursery rhyme
Who stared and stared into the snow until
She saw a diamond, shuddering with light, inside the storm,
I thought that we could see each snowflake wobble through
        the air
And hear them land.
Locked in her room
With yellow flowers on the wallpaper
That wove and welled around her like the snow
Until she almost disappeared in them,
Rapunzel in her cone let down the string the whole world
        could have climbed to save her.
"Oh, don't save me right away," Rapunzel said, "just visit
        me,"
But only dead ones listened to her.
Only the dead could ever visit us this way: locked in a word,
Locked in a world that we can only exorcise, but not convey.

The Hand in the Breast Pocket

1.

My first memory is of the house on Maxim St.
Where we lived in the early '50's.
There was a local haunted house
And a vacant lot where
Dale-girl, Dale-boy and I played on the monkey-bars.
Dale-girl later swallowed a common household poison and
        had to have her stomach pumped.
I remember reading the encyclopedia a lot,
And dreaming of a man in a top-hat with a toilet instead of a
        head.
I remember going to the drive-in wearing my pajamas
And falling asleep.
The first movie I remember seeing
Was *It Came from Outer Space.*

When I was about eight
We moved into a house with a green roof
And a lath-house in the backyard.
It was close to the airport.
I remember lying in bed, listening to the television in the liv-
        ing room
And thinking that the airplanes flying overhead were Russian.
One Christmas I got a bicycle
Which I rode to the seamy side of town where most of the
        horror movies were,

And I had to take piano lessons from a nun who always said
"Hay is for horses"
Whenever I used the word "Hey!"
And I had a microscope,
A BB-gun,
One vicious dog and one kind dog.
When we moved away I kissed the house good-by.

Our next house
—My last house—
Was on the edge of a huge canyon,
With a patio enclosed by sea-green fiberglass.
Manzanita bushes and ice-plant grew up to the garage.
It was 1957, the year of Sputnik,
And I conducted "science experiments" behind the garage,
I.e., set off rockets filled with a mixture of sulphur and zinc
        dust.
Once one of my friends set fire to part of the garage.
I remember taking clarinet lessons
And selling chocolate for the Cody Marching Band
And reading *Tom Sawyer* and all the Sherlock Holmes stories
        over and over every year . . .

2.

Those are my favorite facts,
The facts of a life which now has virtually nothing to do with
       my own.
I wanted to feel the information flow through me like a prism,
To feel the light of everything I had ever done pass through
       me on its way to the rainbow.
This is not memory.
It's more like poking through the trash for something you
       threw away by mistake,
The clarity, the confusion,
The liquid years and now the ones which are like pills.
It's been a long day.
And there aren't any faces in this night,
No real names.

And now each day seems,
Like my own soul, farther and farther off,
Lost in its light as in a dream in which I meant to ask you
       something.
I can feel the life vibrating next to me.
But each day I wear the same clothes,
I say most of the same things,
Somebody listens to them
—Isn't there a moment all this is closing on,

Innocent enough to breathe,
A moment innocent enough to bear its own interpretation?

It's all so natural now,
Everything seems natural.
And I was going to tell you about everything I did today
Leaving none of them out,
The ones whose lives stop here
And about whom there is nothing to say, nothing to look for-
        ward to,
But now I'm not sure that they really exist,
The way I do, in time:
Time is what they do.

When I was ten I had this
Magic eight-ball, filled with black ink
In which an octahedron floated, bearing my eight fortunes on
        its sides.
They were all useless and general;
But they were all true.
And they floated up to the window when I turned it over.

Punchinellos and Dancing Dogs

A tree whose
Boughs are pocket-combs;
A sky as white as a paper
With lots of them on it,
Wearing hats that look like
Truncated ice-cream cones or fezzes,
And wearing masks
With noses that resemble giant facial glands;
One of them jumps through the air with a tambourine;
Another one puffs on a bag of wind,
The King of the Instruments.
Some women are helping them with the noise,
Leaning against a tree
Or a stone, surrounded by dozens of dressed-up dogs
Dancing on their hind legs.

It's a lovely, lonely day,
Another day;
The air is white.
Made out of white air
The punchinellos and their dogs,
The women and the instruments,
The stones, the trees, the hills
And the sky itself are glowing
—A minute or several centuries—
Melting into heavy, wavy lines.